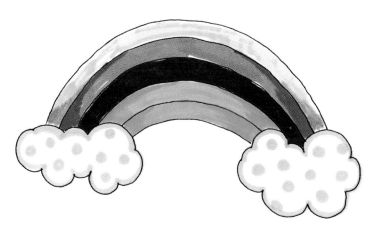

Presented To:

_____

Date:

_____

Little Boys
Activity ✕ Bible
For Toddlers

Little Boys Activity Bible for Toddlers

Copyright © 2002 Educational Publishing Concepts, Inc., Wheaton, IL

Published by New Kids Media ™ in association with Baker Books, a division of Baker Book House Company, P.O. Box 6287, Grand Rapids, MI 49516-6287

Printed in China

Scripture quotations are taken from the Holy Bible, New Living Translation, copyright © 1996. Used by permision of Tyndale House Publishers, Inc. Wheaton, Illinois 60189. All rights reserved.

ISBN 0-8010-4497-9

For current information about all releases from Baker Book House, visit our web site:

http://www.bakerbooks.com

Little Boys Activity Bible For Toddlers

Carolyn Larsen

Illustrated by Caron Turk

BAKER
A DIVISION OF
Baker Book House Co

CONTENTS

Most little boys love making things. What better way to reinforce the stories of the Bible in their young minds, than to make things that will remind them of the stories.

I want to thank Miffy Oakley, a friend who has worked with 2 and 3 year olds for a very long time, for helping me add age-appropriate activities to this book.

Caron–the illustrator, Miffy, and I each hope that you and your little boy enjoy reading these stories, looking for the little floating angel in each illustration, and doing the activities together. We pray that this book brings opportunities for special times of joy as you share the stories of God's love and grow deeper in your love for each other.

Love,
Carolyn Larsen

God Made Everything

Genesis 1-2

Who made the big yellow sun
to warm our days and help
plants grow? **God did!**

Who made the twinkling stars and gentle moon
to cheer up the darkness of night?
God did!

Who made puppies and kittens that run and play? Who made birds that sing and chirp?
God did!

Who made big green trees and small red flowers? Who made tall mountains and rivers and oceans?

God did!

Who made people tall and short? Who made people with blue eyes or brown? Who made all people and loves every one of us?

God!

MOM & ME

Mom: Gather a small flower pot, seeds or a seedling plant, soil, and a watering can.

Me: Work with Mom to plant seeds or a young plant in the flower pot. Help Mom put the soil into the pot, gently plant the seeds, and water it just a bit. Over the next few weeks, watch your plant grow.
Thank God for all the wonderful things he created.

Bad Choices

Genesis 3

God told Adam and Eve not to touch the fruit
of one tree. They could eat all the other fruit in
the Garden of Eden. Eve picked the special
fruit anyway.

Eve took big bite of fruit and juice dripped onto her toes. "Mmmm," she said. It was so good that she wanted Adam to taste it, too.

"God said not to touch this tree," Adam said. He knew that Eve had done something very bad.

"Oh Adam, it's so good. Taste it. You'll like it," Eve kept saying. Adam couldn't resist. He took a bite, too.

God was very sad that Adam and Eve
disobeyed his rule. He made them
leave the beautiful garden. "But,
don't worry," he said. "I still love
you. I'll always love you!"

MOM & ME

Mom: Using markers or paints make a tree trunk on a large piece of white paper. Fill the top of the tree with many branches for your little boy.

Me: Tear pieces of red tissue paper and crumple them into balls. Glue these tissue paper "apples" to the tree branches that Mom made. Share a crisp, juicy apple with Mom while you work.

Noah Obeys

Genesis 6-9

"Noah, there's going to be a flood. Build a big boat," God said. "My friends will make fun of me if I build a boat in my backyard," Noah worried.

"You are the only person who cares about me anymore," God said. "I'm tired of the selfish way people behave. The people who make fun of you will drown in the flood."

23

Noah always tried to obey God, so he got to
work building a boat. He made it just the way
God said. But, just as he thought, his friends
made fun of him.

When the boat was finished, God sent lots of animals to go inside it with Noah's family. Soon they heard rain falling outside. It rained so much that the whole earth flooded.

People everywhere died. When the flood
waters went down, God said, "I'll never send
such a big flood again. This rainbow shows my
promise." Noah thanked God for keeping his
family safe.

MOM & ME

Mom: Gather several small items of different sizes and weights. Fill a sink with water. Stay with your toddler and test which items float and which do not.

Me: Take the things Mom gives you and put them in the water. Do some things float and some things sink? Find one thing that floats and fill it with water. Does it still float?

Baby Laughter

Genesis 18:1-15; 21:1-7

"God said we would have a big family, but, we don't have even one child," Sarah said sadly. She really wanted to be a mother, but now she was very old.

One hot afternoon, three men stopped by Abraham and Sarah's tent to cool off. Sarah served them cool drinks and made dinner for them.

She heard one man say, "By this time next year, Sarah will have a baby." Sarah laughed so hard that she dropped a plate. "At my age, I'm going to have a baby?" she wondered.

"Why is Sarah laughing? Does she think this would be too hard for God?" the man asked. Poor Abraham didn't know what to say.

The man was right! Almost one year later
Abraham and Sarah held their little boy. They
named him Isaac because that name
means, "laughter."

MOM & ME

How much did Abraham and Sarah have to trust God to believe that they could have a baby in their old age? Find out by doing a "trust" exercise of your own.

Mom: Tie a blindfold around your eyes and let your son lead you around the house.

Me: Put on a blindfold and let mom lead you around the house. Talk about what it feels like to trust someone when you can't see where you're going. Talk about the fact that God sees everything and we can trust him with our whole lives.

Making Peace

Genesis 32-33

"Get out! If I ever see you again, you'll be sorry!" Esau shouted at his brother. Jacob had stolen something from him, and Esau was fighting mad!

Now, years later, Jacob was going home. He wondered if his brother was still mad at him. As Jacob and his family traveled, a servant came with some news.

"Your brother is coming to meet you ... and he has an army of 400 men with him," the servant said. Jacob was scared. He was sure that Esau wanted to kill him.

"OK, we'll camp here for the night", Jacob said. "We'll make a present for Esau." Jacob gathered goats, rams, camels, cows, and donkeys to give his brother.

Early the next day his servants took the gifts to Esau. When the brothers finally came face to face, Esau hugged Jacob. "Forget the gifts, I'm just glad to have my brother back," he said.

MOM & ME

Mom: Gather craft materials for your son to make a card.

Me: Talk with Mom about a person with whom you sometimes have trouble getting along—a brother or sister, or maybe a friend. Make a card for that person that will show him or her how much you love them. If you have been fighting with that person, ask Mom to write "I'm sorry" on the card for you, too.

Brotherly Love

Genesis 37, 39-45

"Ha. Dad likes me best!" Joseph teased his
brothers. Their dad had given him a fancy
colorful coat. Joseph's brothers didn't get
anything.

A few days later Joseph's brothers decided to get even. "Let's sell the little troublemaker to those guys going to Egypt. They can sell him to be a slave."

Before Joseph could cry, "Daddy," he was a slave in Egypt. Life wasn't easy there, he even ended up in jail. Through it all, Joseph's faith in God stayed strong.

The Pharaoh had some dreams he didn't understand. God helped Joseph explain the dreams. Pharaoh was so happy that he made Joseph second-in-command of the country.

One day Joseph's brothers came to buy food
from him! Joseph could have thrown them in
jail for being so mean to him. But, he knew God
wanted him to forgive them, so he did.

MOM & ME

Mom: Draw a simple outline of a coat on a piece of paper. Provide various colors of paper for your son to use.

Me: Tear pieces of colored paper, and glue them inside the coat outline that your Mom made. Try to fit the pieces closely together so the coat is filled with many colors.

A Basket Full of Baby

Exodus 2:1-10

"I don't care what Pharaoh orders, I'm not going to let them kill my baby!" Jochebed stomped her foot as she spoke. She MEANT what she said.

Pharaoh had ordered that all Hebrew baby boys be killed. Jochebed had a plan. "Keep your baby brother quiet," she told Miriam. "I'll be back soon."

All baby
BOYS must
be killed!
ORDERED BY
PHAROAH

Jochebed made some long grass into a basket
and covered it with tar. "We'll let it dry," she
said. Miriam had no idea what her
mother was planning.

Later, Jochebed put baby Moses in the basket.
She and Miriam carried it down to the river.
"Take care of my baby, God," Jochebed said
as she gently pushed the basket into the water.

The Egyptian princess found the baby and
decided to keep him. Miriam ran to find
someone to be the baby's nurse. She got her
own mother! God did take care of
Jochebed's baby!

MOM & ME

Mom: Make an area safe for handling modeling clay or Play-Doh–to place where the carpet or furniture
won't be damaged.

Me: Using clay or Play-Doh, make a small basket. Then make a baby to place in the basket. See if the basket will float in a sink full of water. Take it out of the water and let it dry. Then you will always have a basket and baby.

A Hot Message

Exodus 3

"It's been a long day," Moses yawned as he watched his sheep munching on grass. He walked around some to try and wake himself up a bit.

"Whoa! What is that over there? It looks like a bush that's on fire," Moses carefully crossed the meadow to get a better look.

"Moses, take off your shoes. This is holy ground."
Moses stopped where he was. "G-G-God, is
that you?" he asked. The bush kept burning, but
it didn't burn up.

"I have a special job for you," God said. "I want you to go to Egypt and lead my people to freedom. They've been slaves for too long."

Moses took a deep breath. God was asking him to do a big job. At first Moses didn't think he could do it, but he finally said, "I'll do whatever you want me to do, God."

MOM & ME

Mom: Have your little boy stand on a large piece of paper. Trace his bare feet or his shoes.

Me: Color the feet or shoes that Mom traced. Talk about how Moses had to take his shoes off to stand on holy ground.

Backed Up to the Sea

Exodus 14

"Free at last! After 400 years of being slaves, we're finally free!" The Israelites set up camp near the shore of the Red Sea and enjoyed being together.

It wasn't long until their moods changed. "What's that cloud of dust over there?" someone shouted. "I don't know, but it seems to be heading right at us," someone answered.

OH OH

The dust cloud came closer and soon the
Israelites knew it was the Egyptian army.
"Pharaoh sent his soldiers to capture us," the
Israelites cried. "He still wants us to be
his slaves!"

"Moses, what are we going to do?"
Moses stretched his hand out over the Red Sea
and shouted, "Trust God!" The water divided
into two walls.

The Israelites hurried through the
sea . . . walking on dry land!
When the Egyptians
followed, the water walls
crashed down on them.
God saved his people!

MOM & ME

Mom: Gather craft items of a piece of brown construction paper, a piece of blue construction paper, scissors, and glue. Help your son do the gluing and cutting suggested below.

Me: Lay the blue paper on top of the brown paper. Glue the papers together, leaving about 3 inches in the center with no glue. Cut the blue paper from top to bottom. Fold up the cut edges of the blue paper. You now have a dry path through the blue water.

Ten Easy Rules

Exodus 20

Walk, walk, walk. That's all the Israelites had done since leaving Egypt. When Moses said, "Let's camp here," everyone cheered. Moses' wife sat down and rubbed her feet.

"Come up on the mountain, Moses. I want to talk with you," God said. "Don't you even get a chance to rest?" Moses' wife asked. "Do you have to go right now?" He did.

Moses told the people to wait near the mountain while he talked with God. His wife wondered what was happening when thunder boomed and lightning flashed.

Some people hid their eyes. Others shook with fear. Moses' wife was relieved when Moses came back. "What are those stone slabs he's carrying?" she wondered.

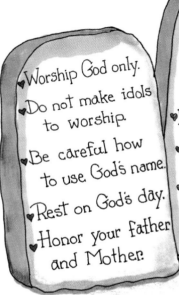

"God wrote ten rules on the stones and gave them to my Moses," she said – so proud. The rules told the people how to live with each other and the best ways to serve God.

MOM & ME

Mom: Cut pieces of paper to resemble stone tablets.

Me: Help Mom say the Ten Commandments in short words. Mom will write them on the stone tablet papers. Decorate the edges of the tablets. Hang them on your refrigerator to remind your whole family of them.

The Talking Donkey

Numbers 22:21-34

King Balak wanted Balaam to put a curse on the God's people. God didn't want Balaam to do it. He said, "Don't go to the king." Balaam went anyway.

He was riding along when all of a sudden his donkey ran off the road. "What's wrong with you?" Balaam shouted. He hit the donkey and dragged it back to the road.

A few minutes later, the donkey ran right into a
building, hurting Balaam's leg. A while later, it
just sat down in the road and wouldn't budge.
Balaam was mad!

Balaam beat his donkey until it turned around and said, "Why are you hitting me? I'm trying to protect you." A talking donkey? Balaam didn't know what to think.

Then, he saw what the donkey had seen—an angel, holding a sword. "I was disobeying God and you saved me from his anger!" Balaam cried, hugging the donkey's neck.

MOM & ME

Balaam had to learn a lesson about obeying because he tried to do something that God told him not to do.

Play an obeying game called "Mother, May I?" You stand at one side of the room. Mom stands at the other side. Mom will say, "You may take 2 steps forward (or some amount of steps). Before you can move, you must say, "Mother, may I?" If you forget, you must return to the starting point. The goal is to get across the room to where Mom stands. When you succeed, let Mom have a turn.

The Walls of Jericho

Joshua 6

And the walls came a tumblin' down

Do you think that big stone walls could fall down just because some people marched around them a few times? That's what happened in Jericho.

"God says to march around Jericho once a day for six days. If we do what he says, he will help us capture the city," Joshua told the Israelite army.

"We can't say anything or even talk to each other while we march. The only sound will be the priests blowing their horns." The people thought this was a strange plan.

Once a day for six days the Israelites marched around Jericho. The people living inside the city made fun of them. They thought the Israelites were crazy.

On the seventh day, the Israelites marched
around Jericho seven times. On the last trip
around the priests blew the horns, the people
shouted and the big walls tumbled down! The
Israelites captured the city without
even a fight!

MOM & ME

Mom: Help your son build a "wall" using blocks.

Me: Build a wall using your blocks. Make it as high as you can. Make it thick by using two rows of blocks. Talk about how the Israelites had to march around the walls of Jericho many times, just the way God told them to, before the wall fell. Then, make your wall fall down.

A Second Chance

Judges 16

"God, please give me one more chance to serve you," Samson prayed. "Please! I know I messed up before, but I want to do what's right now."

Samson was the strongest man who ever lived.
He killed animals with his bare hands. He won
every fight he had with God's enemies,
the Philistines.

One day he wasn't paying attention and the
Philistines captured him. "You aren't so mighty
now, are you?" they teased, while they
tied him up.

One day the Philistines planned a big party. "What can we do to entertain the people?" they wondered. "Let's bring Samson out and make fun of him. The people will love that!"

That was the day Samson prayed for a second
chance. God answered his prayer and gave
his strength back. Samson pushed against the
columns of the big building and the ceiling
crashed down. It killed Samson ... and
all the Philistines.

MOM & ME

Mom: Gather several items of various weights for your son to try a weight-lifting experiment. Get a bathroom scale to measure the weight of the items.

Me: Samson was very strong–the strongest man alive. Do you think that you are very strong, too? Lift some of the items Mom has gathered. What is the heaviest one that you can lift by yourself? Can you lift a heavier one with Mom's help?

God Speaks
to Samuel

1 Samuel 3

Samuel was trying to sleep, but someone was
calling his name. Samuel lived in the temple. Eli,
the priest, was teaching him how to serve God.

When Samuel went to bed, he fell right asleep.
Then he heard someone call him. He hopped
out of bed and ran to see what Eli wanted.

But, it wasn't Eli who called him. He wasn't very
happy to be awakened, either. Samuel went
back to bed. He was almost asleep when
someone called him again.

Three times Samuel heard someone call him.
Each time he ran to Eli. Finally, Eli knew that it
was God calling young Samuel.

God called again and Samuel answered just
the way Eli said he should. God told Samuel
important things about the future.

MOM & ME

Game time! Pretend that you are sleeping.
Mom will stand in the next room and whisper
your name. How close does Mom have to be
to you before you can hear her whisper? After
you hear Mom's whisper, let her try hearing you
whisper her name.

God's Big Power

I Samuel 3

See that giant soldier? He is Goliath. He's nine feet tall. He has a big spear and a big shield ... and he's mean. King Saul's soldiers are afraid of him.

"Send someone to fight me, you chickens. Surely your God will help you win," Goliath shouted every day. Not one soldier volunteered.

"I'll fight the giant!" David announced. "You're too little," King Saul said. David wasn't afraid, though. He knew God would help him.

David picked up stones on his way down the hill. He pulled his slingshot out of his pocket. King Saul's soldiers hid behind trees and rocks. They thought David was in big trouble.

"Come on, kid. I'll feed you to the birds," Goliath
growled. David put a stone in his sling and
threw it at Goliath. It smacked the giant right in
the head and he fell down ... dead! God
helped David win!

MOM & ME

Mom: Gather some empty tin cans or empty paper towel cardboard tubes. You will also need a small soft foam ball, or balls made of crumpled paper.

Me: David had a good aim to be able to hit the giant with his slingshot, didn't he? Do you have a good aim, too? Set up the cans or cardboard tubes on the edge of a table. Stand far enough way from the table that you have to aim at the items. Throw your ball or paper at the cans or tubes. Can you knock them down?

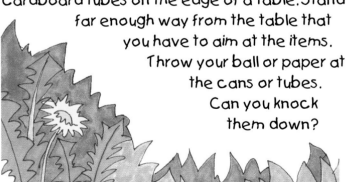

Fire on the Mountain

I Kings 18:19-40

"I challenge you to a contest!" Elijah shouted. "We'll see who the real God is!" There were about 400 followers of Baal. Only Elijah stood for God.

Baal's followers built an altar and put a bull on it. Then they danced around and shouted for Baal to send fire down and burn up the offering. Nothing happened.

Elijah sat under a tree and watched them.
"Maybe your god is on vacation. Maybe he's
sleeping, or in the bathroom." He let them try all
day to get Baal's attention.

"OK, enough," Elijah said. "My turn." He built an altar and had four big jars of water poured over it. The whole thing was floating in water!

"God, show these men that you are the real and true God," he prayed. Fire shot down from the sky. It burned up the altar, the bull, and all the water!

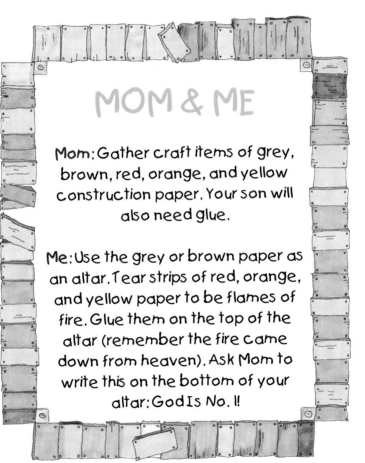

MOM & ME

Mom: Gather craft items of grey, brown, red, orange, and yellow construction paper. Your son will also need glue.

Me: Use the grey or brown paper as an altar. Tear strips of red, orange, and yellow paper to be flames of fire. Glue them on the top of the altar (remember the fire came down from heaven). Ask Mom to write this on the bottom of your altar: God Is No. 1!

The Chariot of Fire

2 Kings 2:1-18

Elisha wanted to learn everything he could
about serving God. He followed Elijah
everywhere. "Teach me all you know,"
he begged Elijah.

People constantly asked Elisha, "Did you know that God is going to take your master away very soon?" Elisha did know and he tried to learn a lot from Elijah.

One day Elijah slapped his jacket on the water of the Jordan River. Water splashed on Elisha as the waters divided. They walked through on dry ground.

"I want to be God's prophet like you are," Elisha begged. "If you see me leave this earth, then God will give you what you ask," Elijah answered.

Just then, a chariot made of fire zoomed down from heaven. Elijah got in it and was taken to heaven. Elisha saw the whole thing. He became the next prophet of God.

MOM & ME

Mom: Bring out photo albums of older family members.

Me: Look at a picture of your grandparents and even your great-grandparents. Can you think of something you have learned from someone who is older than you are? Can Mom remember something she learned how to do by listening to an older person?

Cauliflower, Carrots, and Courage

Daniel 1

King Nebuchadnezzar took many Israelite boys as prisoners. He put them in a special training program to learn how to be palace workers.

The boys were treated well. They were served the best food in the kingdom. Most of the boys thought the program was great. They enjoyed the fancy meals.

Daniel, Shadrach, Meshach, and Abednego
didn't want to eat the food. It was offered to
idols before it was served to them. They didn't
want to do anything that didn't honor God.

"Please, let us have vegetables and water for ten days," Daniel begged the guard. If we aren't healthier than the other boys, then we'll eat the king's food."

Praise God

The guard agreed to the test. After ten days,
Daniel and his friends were the strongest and
healthiest of all. God took care of them
because they honored him.

MOM & ME

Enjoy a healthy snack together.

Mom: Supply a healthy snack. Talk about how
important it is to put healthy things in our bodies
so they can be strong and do all the things
they are supposed to do.
Me: Ask Mom what she thinks your body would
be like if you only ate cookies and candy.

The Fiery Furnace

Daniel 3

"Bow down and worship this statue of me," King
Nebuchadnezzar ordered. Most people did,
but Shadrach, Meshach, and Abednego
refused. They worshiped only God.

The king got very angry with the three boys.
"Arrest them! Heat the furnace up seven times
hotter than normal. Throw them into it!"
he shouted.

"Our God will take care of us," the three boys said. King Nebuchadnezzar didn't believe them. He sat down in front of the furnace to watch them burn.

"Wait a minute," the king cried. "I see four boys in the fire instead of three." The fourth person was God's angel. "Get them out here," the king shouted.

"God kept us safe!" the boys cried. "We said he would!" The king ordered everyone in the kingdom to respect God.

MOM & ME

Mom: Cut a simple angel from a piece of white paper. Provide craft items of glue, colored glue, glitter, and markers.

Me: Decorate the angel that Mom cut out. When you are finished, put it somewhere near your bed to remind you that God is always taking care of you.

Daniel and the Lions' Den

Daniel 6

"Did you hear that King Darius is going to make Daniel our boss?" one man asked. "Daniel is a slave. He shouldn't be a boss. We have to get rid of him."

The jealous men looked for ways to get Daniel in trouble with the king. They decided to get him in trouble for praying to his God every day.

Let's get Daniel in trouble...

Daniel prays only to God!

New Law...
All people must pray to me!
the King

They tricked the king into making a law that people could pray only to him. Of course, Daniel ignored it and continued praying to God. That's what the mean men counted on.

They jumped on Daniel when he was praying. Before he knew it he was in the middle of a bunch of hungry lions. That was the punishment for disobeying the king's law.

PRAISE GOD!

God protected Daniel because he hadn't done anything wrong. The lions didn't touch him. The next day the king shouted, "Hurray for Daniel's God! Everyone should worship him!"

MOM & ME

Mom: Provide a piece of construction paper, folded in half. Ask your son to lay his hand on the paper, with his little finger on the fold. Trace his hand.

Me: Decorate the outside of your hand outline. On the inside, ask Mom to help you write down a list of things you like to pray for.

A Fishy Lesson

Jonah 1-4

"I don't like the people in Nineveh. I don't want to tell them about God!" Jonah shouted. He hopped on a boat heading away from Nineveh. "God will never find me here!" he thought.

Jonah was sleeping when a big storm blew up.
The sailors were afraid their boat would sink.
"Get up! If you have a god, pray to him. We're in
big trouble!" a sailor shouted.

Jonah knew the storm was his fault. "Throw me overboard and the storm will stop," he said. The sailors tossed Jonah into the sea and the storm stopped.

A big fish swallowed Jonah right away. He had three days of time-out in the fish to think about how he disobeyed God.

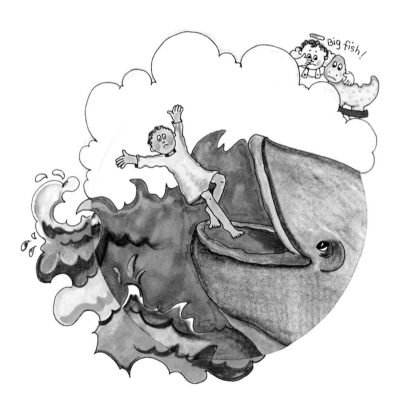

'I'm sorry, God. I'll go to Nineveh if you want
me to go," he decided. The fish spit him out and
he went straight to Nineveh to tell
about God's love.

MOM & ME

Mom: Draw and cut out a simple fish shape. Make it as large as you can. Cut several small doors in the fish, leaving one side attached so the door can open and close. Draw a simple stick figure of Jonah that will fit behind each door.

Me: Ask Mom to hide her eyes, then you hide Jonah behind one of the doors in the big fish. Ask Mom to guess where Jonah is hiding. When she finds him, let her hide the Jonah figure and you guess where he is hiding.

John the Baptist Is Born

Luke 1:5-25, 57-64

I saw an angel!!

Zechariah had exciting news, but he couldn't tell anyone! God took his voice away because he didn't believe a message from God's angel. He saw an angel ... and he couldn't tell anyone!

Zechariah made up some sign language that his wife, Elizabeth, understood. "God said we're going to have a baby? You're kidding, right? I'm too old to have a baby."

The angel said their boy would tell the world
that the Messiah was coming! Elizabeth had so
many questions, but Zechariah's voice
wouldn't come back until the baby was born.

Many relatives had ideas for the new parents. "What are you going to name him?" "It should be Zechariah." "No, he should have your father's name."

what is his name?

Zechariah grabbed a tablet and scratched, "His name is John. That's what the angel said to name him." Immediately Zechariah could speak again!

MOM & ME

Can you imagine not being able to talk for almost a year? See how long you can go without talking by playing The Quiet Game. You may use sign language and any other way to say what you want to say—except talking. See how long you can be completely quiet! Make it a contest with Mom to see who can be quiet the longest.

A Very Special Baby

Matthew 1:20-25; Luke 2:1-20

"Joseph," the angel whispered, "Mary was telling
the truth. She is going to have a baby. The baby
is the Son of God. Go ahead and marry her.
Take care of her."

Joseph and Mary did get married. When it was time for the baby to be born, they had to go to Bethlehem to be counted in a census. It was a bumpy donkey ride for Mary.

"We'll be there soon, Mary," Joseph promised.
"I'll get a nice room and you can sleep while I
take care of business." That sounded
good to Mary.

When they got to Bethlehem, Joseph searched and searched. There were no rooms left in the whole town. The best he could get was a spot in a stable where Mary could rest.

no more room!

Later that night, baby Jesus was born. Angels announced his birth to shepherds out in the field. They hurried to town to see the baby Son of God!

MOM & ME

Mom: Get a package of pre-made cookie dough, a rolling pin, an angel-shaped cookie cutter, a baking sheet, and some frosting and other cookie decorations that your son likes.

Me: Help Mom roll out the cookie dough and cut out some angel-shaped cookies. Bake the cookies. When the cookies are cool, decorate them with frosting and the other decorations your Mom has.

Keeping Jesus Safe

Matthew 2:1-23

Joseph, Mary and Jesus stayed in Bethlehem.
Jesus grew to be a happy little boy. Joseph
worked as a carpenter. Things were fine until
one night.

"Joseph, wake up," an angel whispered. "You have to get Jesus out of here. Some people want to hurt him." Joseph jumped up and quickly woke Mary.

They grabbed a few things and left Bethlehem. Mary rode on the donkey with Jesus sleeping in her arms. The next morning, their friends didn't know where they were.

The little family went to Egypt. It was hard because the people there spoke a different language and had different customs. They even worshiped a different god.

One night the angel came back to Joseph. "You
can go home now. The people who wanted to
hurt Jesus are dead." They were so happy
to go home.

MOM & ME

Joseph was a carpenter. Jesus probably learned how to be a carpenter, too. What are some things that a carpenter does? One thing a carpenter does is hammer nails into wood.

Mom: Get a piece of scrap wood, some small nails and a lightweight hammer. Hammer the nail part way into the wood. Let your son finish the job.

Me: Finish pounding the nail into the wood. Be careful to keep your fingers away from where the hammer is hitting.

Jesus Goes Fishing

Luke 5:1-11

Peter was cleaning his fishing nets. He and his friends had fished all night without catching anything. He wanted to go home and get some sleep.

"Can I stand in your boat to teach these people?" Jesus asked Peter. Hundreds of people were pushing each other to get close to Jesus.

Jesus climbed into the boat and Peter pushed
it out a little way into the lake. He listened as
Jesus taught the people about God.

When the people left, Jesus said, "Throw your nets there and you will catch fish." He pointed to the spot where Peter had fished all night without catching anything.

Peter threw his net into the water. It filled up
with hundreds of fish. Peter was surprised. Jesus
smiled and said, "Follow me and I will teach you
to fish for people instead of fish."

MOM & ME

Mom: Make a fishing pole by tying a piece of string on the end of a dowel rod. Bend a paper clip into a hook shape and attach it to the end of the string. Bend other paper clips into a hook shape and lay them on the floor.

Me: Hold the fishing pole that Mom made. See if you can hook any of the "fish" that are laying on the floor.

Jesus Calms the Storm

Luke 8:22-25

"How does Jesus keep going? He's been teaching all day. I've just been listening to him, but I'm tired!" Peter said with a big yawn.

"He's finishing up," John answered. Jesus came over to his friends and told them that he wanted to go across the lake.

When they got into the boat, Jesus fell right to sleep. Pretty soon a strong wind blew up. The little boat bounced around on the waves. The disciples were afraid.

"Jesus, wake up! We're going to drown!" Peter shook Jesus shoulders. Jesus stood up and shouted, "Be quiet!" The wind and rain stopped immediately.

He looked around sadly at his friends. "Where is
your faith?" he asked. The disciples had no
doubt now that Jesus was God's Son.

MOM & ME

Mom: Get an empty jar that has a screw-on lid, water, vegetable oil, and food coloring.

Me: Fill the jar half full of water, and add an equal amount of vegetable oil. Add a few drops of food coloring. Put on the lid and shake the jar. Now you can shake the jar hard and make stormy waves, or shake it gently to make small waves.

Feeding 5,000 People

John 6:1-13

"Mom! My friends are going to hear Jesus teach. Can I go? Huh, can I?" the little boy begged. "Sure, just let me pack you a little lunch," his mom answered.

The boy and his friends found a spot close to the front of the crowd of thousands of people. Jesus taught all day and the boy listened closely to each word.

Late in the day one man said, "Send the people
home for dinner." Jesus answered, "No, you give
them dinner." The man mumbled back, "We
don't have any food."

The little boy held out his lunch and said, "You can have this, if it will help." Jesus' friend shook his head, but Jesus smiled. "Thank you," he said, and he took the lunch.

Jesus prayed for the food and the disciples passed it out to the people. More than 5,000 people had all they wanted to eat ... and there was some left over. It all came from one little lunch.

PRAISE God

MOM & ME

Mom: Supply fish crackers, a favorite kind of regular cracker, and juice boxes.

Me: Invite a friend to go with you and Mom for a picnic lunch of fish and bread.

Jesus Walks on Water

Matthew 14:22-33

It was a stormy night. Rain pounded against the boat. The wind blew waves up high. The men on the boat were scared of the storm.

"I wish Jesus was here," one man said. Everyone agreed, but there was no time to talk about it. It took all their energy to bail water out of the boat.

"Hey, what's that?" someone shouted. "It looks like someone walking on the water, but that's crazy!" "Don't be afraid," a voice shouted, "it's me, Jesus!"

"If it's really you," Peter shouted, "let me walk to you on top of the water."
"Come on," Jesus shouted. Peter leapt out of the boat and ran across the water.

Praise God!

Then, he took his eyes off Jesus ...
and he sank into the water. "HELP!"
he screamed. Instantly, Jesus lifted him out of
the water and helped him into the boat.

MOM & ME

Only Jesus could walk on water . . . or help someone walk on water. But, you can certainly enjoy water. Play your favorite water games: Use a sprinkling can or spray bottle, and play in the sprinkler outside. If it's too cold to play in water outside, gather all your favorite bathtub toys and play in the bathtub.

The Good Samaritan

Luke 10:30-37

"I'm going to Jericho," the man called to his wife. It was a nice day for a walk. He enjoyed the sunshine and the singing birds. He even hummed a tune as he walked.

When he rounded a bend in the road, a couple of robbers jumped him. They beat him up, stole his money, and even took his clothes, then left him to die.

The man thought he was saved when he saw a priest coming down the road. But the priest crossed the road to get away from the hurt man.

Later a temple worker came by. He didn't help the man either. After that the man thought he was going to die. He heard footsteps again, but when he saw it was a Samaritan, he gave up hope.

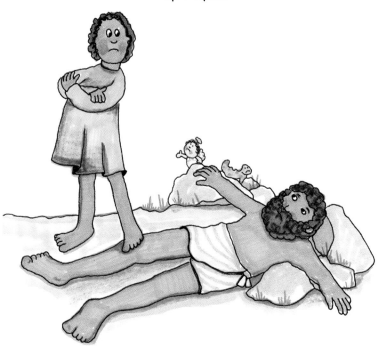

Samaritans hated Jews, so it was surprising
that the Samaritan cleaned the hurt man's
wounds and took him to an inn to rest and get
well. The Samaritan showed God's love to the
hurt man.

MOM & ME

Mom: Supply "bandages" by tearing old sheets or towels into strips. If you don't' have bandages, supply Band-Aids™ and towels to use for slings.

Me: The man in the story was hurt very badly. The Good Samaritan helped him by bandaging his wounds. Can you bandage Mom's pretend cuts and scrapes. Ask Mom to bandage your pretends cuts and injuries.

The Prodigal Son

Luke 15:11-32

"I'm tired of this farm! When you die I'll get some of your money, so just give it to me now," the young boy said to his father. "Then I can leave this farm."

The father watched sadly as his son left with pockets full of money. The boy spent money wildly in the city. He threw parties and bought presents for people.

Before he knew it, all his money was gone. So were all the people who were supposedly his friends. The boy had no place to live and no food to eat.

The only job he could find was feeding pigs. "Even the hired workers on my dad's farm have more money than I do," he thought. "Maybe Dad would give me a job."

Every day since his son left, the father
watched for him to come home. When he saw
his son coming, he ran to meet him. The father
threw a big party to welcome his son home.

MOM & ME

Mom: Gather books that have pictures of animals and books or magazines with pictures of people.

Me: Look at the pictures of animals. Where do the animals live? What kinds of things do they eat? What do they do all day? Where do they sleep? Now look at the pictures of people. Answer the same questions about the people. Which way would you rather live?

Saying Thank You

Luke 17:11-19

"Jesus, help us! Please help us!" Jesus looked around to see who was calling him. He saw ten men who were sick with leprosy.

People with leprosy had to stay away from healthy people. They couldn't live with their families. The sick people were called "lepers" and lived together outside of town. It was a lonely life.

Jesus called to the ten
men, "Go show yourselves
to the priests." All the
lepers ran to town. As they
were running something
amazing happened.

Thank you, Jesus

"Hey, I can feel my fingers!" one shouted.
"Yeah, the white spots on my leg are gone!" said
another. "We're healed! Jesus did it! He made us
well!" they cheered.

Jesus healed them!

Nine men ran to town. One man went back to Jesus. "Thank you for healing me," he said. Jesus wished the other nine men had thanked him too.

MOM & ME

Mom: Supply craft items like poster board, markers, glue, and magazines from which to cut pictures.

Me: Make a "Thank You" Poster. Look through the magazines to find pictures of things you are thankful for. Have Mom cut out those pictures and you glue them on the poster board. Decorate the top and sides of the poster using the markers.

Zacchaeus

Luke 19:1-10

"Out of my way! Move!" Zacchaeus shouted.
People lined the street to see Jesus.
Zacchaeus was a tax collector. No one liked
him, so no one paid any attention to him.

Zacchaeus could hear people coming down the street. He leaned against a big sycamore tree to think of something to do. That gave him an idea.

Zacchaeus quickly climbed up the tree and scooted out to the middle of one of the big branches. Now he was sitting right over the road where Jesus would pass by.

Zacchaeus was surprised when Jesus looked up at him and said, "Come down. I want to come to your house today."

After talking with Jesus, Zacchaeus knew it was wrong to cheat people. He promised to pay back everyone he had cheated.

MOM & ME

Mom: Draw a tree on a piece of construction paper. Cut out several large green leaves. Draw a stick figure Zacchaeus that is smaller than some of the leaves.

Me: Glue the leaves on the tree that Mom drew. Leave one part of each leaf loose. Hide Zacchaeus under a leaf and see if Mom can find him. When she does, then let her hide Zacchaeus and you find him.

Four Good Friends

Mark 2:3-12

This poor man
is paralyzed.
That means
he can't stand up or walk. His legs don't work.
He gets lonely, but he has four very good
friends who visit him.

"I wish we could help our friend," one man said. "I have an idea," another answered. "Jesus is in town. He heals sick people, maybe he will help our friend."

The friends made a special cot with rope
handles on each corner. They put their friend
on it and took him to the house where Jesus
was teaching."

The house was so crowded that they couldn't get in. "Please let us get our friend to Jesus," they cried. But, no one would move. So the friends came up with a new plan.

They carried their friend to the top of the
house, dug a hole in the roof, and lowered his
cot down in front of Jesus. Everyone was
amazed, but Jesus saw their faith. He made
their friend well so he could walk!

MOM & ME

Mom: Supply a blanket and a stuffed animal.

Me: Put your stuffed animal in the blanket. You hold two corners of the blanket and ask Mom to hold two corners. Carry the blanket around the house, pretending that you are taking the stuffed animal to Jesus.

Jesus Dies

John 19:16-30

where are your friends?

Jesus' friends ran when the soldiers arrested Jesus. A quick trial was held, but Jesus' friends weren't there. Angry people said Jesus was so bad he should be killed.

"Move!" a soldier growled at Jesus. The soldier cracked a whip in the air over Jesus' head. The soldier made Jesus pick up a heavy wooden cross and carry it down the street.

A crowd of people followed
Jesus to the hill outside of
town. The soldiers threw
Jesus down on the ground
and put him on a big cross.
They killed him.

Jesus' friends were in the crowd. They didn't understand why some people were so angry with Jesus. He was always kind and loving. He had never hurt anyone.

Jesus' friends were so sad when
he died. A man named Joseph
took Jesus' body and buried it
on his land, in a place called
a "tomb."

MOM & ME

Mom: Supply materials to make three crosses. Use popsicle sticks, twigs, or heavy paper and glue. Also supply a small flower pot filled with soil.

Me: Make three crosses, using the materials Mom supplies. Put the crosses in the flower pot and leave it where it will be a daily reminder of the fact that Jesus died because he loves you.

The Resurrection

Mark 16:1-7

It was early Sunday morning. Some women
were up early and already busy. They were
friends of Jesus and they had something
important to do.

The women were on their way to the tomb where Jesus was buried. They were going to put perfumes and oils on Jesus' body. That was their custom.

"How are we going to move the big stone in front of the tomb door?" one woman asked. The soldiers had put it there. It was very big and heavy.

"We'll figure out something," another woman said. When they got to the tomb, the stone was already moved! An angel stepped out of the tomb with a surprising message.

"You're looking for Jesus," the angel said. "He's
not here. He came back to life, just as he said
he would." The women danced and shouted,
"He's alive! Jesus is alive!"

MOM & ME

Mom: Supply construction paper, a metal brad and markers.

Me: Make a tomb that has a round stone in front of it. Attach the stone to the tomb using the brad. Now you can roll the stone away. Decorate the outside of the tomb by making flowers and bushes with the markers.

The Best Gift

Acts 3:1-10

This man couldn't walk. Every day his friends carried him to this same spot. He spent the day begging other people for money. He wasn't a very happy man.

Every day the man begged money from the people going in and out of Jerusalem. That's the only way he could buy food.

"Money for the poor?" he called out to all who
passed by. "Sir," a voice interrupted his begging.
The man looked up to see two men standing in
front of him.

He held out his hand for money, but Peter said, "We don't have any money. We have something better than money to give you."

"In the name of Jesus, get up and walk," Peter
continued. Instantly, the man's legs were
better. He got up and walked home, praising
God all the way.

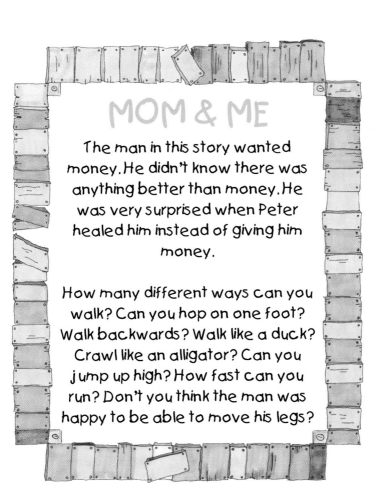

MOM & ME

The man in this story wanted money. He didn't know there was anything better than money. He was very surprised when Peter healed him instead of giving him money.

How many different ways can you walk? Can you hop on one foot? Walk backwards? Walk like a duck? Crawl like an alligator? Can you jump up high? How fast can you run? Don't you think the man was happy to be able to move his legs?

Philip and the Chariot Race

Acts 8:26-40

"Philip," the angel said, "go south down the desert road that goes from Jerusalem to Gaza." Philip didn't even ask why. He left right away.

Pretty soon Philip saw a fancy chariot racing toward him. As it flew past, he saw an important man from Ethiopia inside. The Holy Spirit told Philip to catch the chariot.

Philip ran so fast that he caught up to the chariot. The man inside was reading from the book of Isaiah. "Do you understand what you're reading?" Philip asked.

"How could I? No one has explained it to me,"
the man answered. "I can tell you what it
means," Philip said. He climbed into the
carriage and taught the man.

Philip can explain it!

He explained the whole story of God's love.
"Stop the chariot!" the Ethiopian shouted. "I
believe what you are saying. I want to be
baptized right here."

MOM & ME

The man in the chariot wasn't reading a Bible like we have today. He was probably reading a scroll.

Mom: Supply a piece of construction paper or white paper and a marker.

Me: Make a scroll by rolling the paper up into a tube shape. Before you roll it up, ask Mom to write, "Jesus loves you!" on the scroll.

GAZA

Jerusalem

Paul's Changed Life

Acts 9:1-20

"I hate Christians!" Saul shouted. He spent his life arresting Christians and putting them in jail. He wanted to stop people from hearing about Jesus.

One day Saul decided to go to Damascus to arrest Christians there, too. Along the road Saul heard a voice ask, "Why are you hurting me and troubling me?"

A bright light shined onto
Saul. "Why are you hurting me?"
the voice asked again. Saul didn't
see anyone around. His friends didn't see
anyone either.

"Who are you?" Saul asked. "I am Jesus," the voice answered. Now Saul knew that all the stories about Jesus were true. He was sorry for hurting Christians.

Saul's heart changed. He believed in Jesus ...now he was a Christian, too. God changed Saul's name to Paul. Paul spent the rest of his life preaching about God's love.

MOM & ME

Mom: Supply a sheet of white paper a sheet of black paper, and a marker. Cut large hearts from these papers that are exactly the same size.

Me: Glue the black heart and white heart together. Use a marker to make a cross on the white side. Talk about how Paul's heart changed from black to white when he believed in Jesus.

Peter in Prison

Acts 12:6-17

Peter wanted to go to sleep, but he couldn't get comfortable because he was chained between two guards. Peter was in prison because he taught other people about Jesus.

Four squads of four soldiers each stood guard outside Peter's cell. King Herod didn't want him to escape! Peter finally fell asleep, but he didn't sleep well.

He woke up when something jabbed him in the side. A bright angel stood in front of him. "Get up," the angel said. The chains fell off Peter's arms and legs.

The angel led Peter past the guards and out of
the prison. At first, Peter thought he was
dreaming. When he was safely on the street,
he knew this wasn't a dream. He was free!

The angel disappeared, and Peter hurried to a house where his friends were praying for his safety. He told them that their prayers had been answered.

MOM & ME

Mom: Supply several strips of construction paper that are five inches long and one inch wide. Also supply glue.

Me: Glue the strips of paper together to make a chain. Put the last circle on each end around your wrists. Now, your hands are chained together like Peter. Ask Mom to read the story to you again. When she reads how the chains fell off Peter's arms, break the chains around your wrists. Hooray! Your free!

Prison Earthquake

Acts 16:16-40

The jailer shoved Paul and Silas into the dark cell in the middle of the prison. They were in big trouble. They might even be killed.

Paul and Silas sat on the dirty floor of the cell and sang songs about God. They wanted the other prisoners to know how much God loved them.

The songs made the other prisoners feel better. Around midnight, the floor of the prison started shaking. The prisoners wondered what was happening.

It shook harder. The walls started crumbling. The chains holding prisoners broke. The door fell open. The prisoners started to escape!

Paul kept the prisoners there and the jailer was so relieved! He could have been in big trouble if his prisoners left. "How can I be a Christian, too?" he asked. Paul and Silas told his whole family about Jesus, and they all became Christians.

"Praise God"

MOM & ME

Mom: Make a small red heart from construction paper. Supply glue and the materials to make a cross—wooden sticks or brown paper. While your son is gluing the red heart on the cross, explain to him that all people do bad things ... and this is called "sin." Because of sin, we can't live in heaven with God. But, Jesus loves us so much that he died on the cross for our sins. He didn't stay dead, but he came back to life and lives in heaven again. Everyone who believes in all that Jesus did, can live in heaven with God someday.

Me: Make a cross and glue the red heart right in the middle of it.

A Little Boy Helps

Acts 23:1-35

"Put Paul in jail!" a man called. "If you don't,
these people will kill him." People were mad at
Paul because he taught that people could live
in heaven someday.

The next day some men made plans to murder Paul. They each promised not to eat or drink until Paul was dead. They didn't know that a boy overheard their plan.

The boy was Paul's nephew and he ran to the
prison to tell his uncle about the plan. Paul
listened carefully. He knew exactly what to do.

"Take this boy to the commander. He has important news," Paul told a guard. The boy was scared, but he loved his uncle, so he told the commander what he had heard.

The commander sent Paul to Caesarea where he would be safe. Nearly 500 men guarded him on the way. The boy was glad he had helped Uncle Paul.

MOM & ME

This boy was a big help to Paul, wasn't he? He was also very brave. Just in case you think sometimes little kids can't really do things to help others, make a list of helping things to do.

Mom: Supply a piece of white paper. Trace your little boy's hand on the paper.

Me: What ways can I help others? Write down ideas on the "Helping Hand."